Y0-BCO-017

THIS WOMA

S.C. 811.54 FREE Copy 3

Freeman, Grace Beacham.

This woman called mother

South Carolina State Library
Columbia, S.C.

Books by Grace Beacham Freeman:
NO COSTUMES OR MASKS
MIDNIGHT TO DAWN
NOT SET IN STONE
THIS WOMAN CALLED MOTHER
CHILDREN ARE POETRY (Envelope Book)
STARS AND THE LAND (Chapbook)

THIS WOMAN CALLED MOTHER

by
Grace Beacham Freeman

 ST. ANDREWS PRESS
Laurinburg, North Carolina
1992

Acknowledgements

This Woman Called Mother has been a long time in its birthing. Some of those who were active midwives or who made valuable suggestions on how these poems should be cradled are Susan Ludvigson, Michelle and Neil Covington, Gaylon and Peter Syrett , Elizabeth Ellison and Scharme Price. Especially helpful, too, were our daughter Katharine Parker and her daughter Holly and, of course, my husband, John. Without his insistant but gentle nagging to get on with it, this book would still be in an early gestation stage.

Special thanks go to critic and friend Arla Holroyd who not only nurtures and disciplines me, but other poets as well.

We thank Charles Loftin for the use of his sensitive drawing on the cover.

Several of the poems, some with changes in title or content, have appeared previously in *St. Andrews Review, The Faces of Appalachia, Appalachia - Land and People, No Costumes or Masks, Midnight to Dawn* and *Not Set In Stone.*

© 1992 Grace Beacham Freeman

St. Andrews Press
St. Andrews College
Laurinburg, N. C.

ISBN 1-879934-03-5

In Memory of
Grace Bailey Beacham
role model for much of my mothering
and my good feelings about being a woman
and wife to John

CONTENTS

"Daughters seldom know their mothers as women, only as nurturers."

RITUAL OF THE APPLE

A slim two blade affair,
it folded neatly into itself
from rounded silver ends
good for hammering tacks
into kitchen walls for
pictures my snub nosed
crayons endlessly produced;
for sounding out the safeness
of canned foods by tapping
the centers of metal tops;
for rapping smartly but gently
on window glass
to see if folks whose doorbells
did not work were home.

My father's pocket knife sported
a small silver shield imbedded
in its black bone handle,
mute evidence that it could,
under real duress,
become a weapon of sorts --
a sword unsheathed in my defense?
The only time I saw it bring blood
was when its scalpel-sharp small blade
probed for a stubborn splinter
in my mother's trembling finger.

Still, we knew,
my mother and I,
we were safe
when my father
and his pocket knife were near.

But my father's real talent
lay in peeling an apple.
He polished its skin to a high shine
with his hands and leg of his pants.
Only when it was bright and shiny as
the brass door knobs
my mother took such pride in
did he reach for his pocket knife.

Holding and turning the glossy apple
first at eye level, as though sighting
for proper lighting,
he would pierce the gleaming skin
and begin the gorgeous unbroken curl
of peel for me to swirl and
dance with until it broke
and I sank into a chair ready to consume
the glistening slices my mother had arranged
like a flower in a juicy circle.

The ritual over for me,
I was willingly led to bed
and tucked inside my
cocoon of blankets.

Not until now,
this poem even,
can I conceive
this woman called mother
returning to my father as Eve,
dancing,
an apple in her hand.

LAUGHTER

Laughter is a bell ringing
bringing those in earshot together.
Like weather, it is free.
Join in,
join in!

Laughter is a balm,
calming frenzied tempers,
relaxing knotted minds,
healing egos
aching for attention.

Laughter is a whip.
Its lashes bruise deep.
No court punishes those
who use it on children
or old people in their care.

Laughter has many faces.
Only with the very young,
staring eye to eye,
or the very old,
too tired to pretend,
can it be trusted.

PROBE

Why am I weeping, Mother?
I do not remember your eyes wet.
For me, they always mirrored laughter --
bubbly as the fizz of gingerale
that was our house champagne
and tempting as the opened box
of chocolate covered cherries,
sweet staple of our celebrating.
Without it,
would we recognize each other?

In this search for the woman
inside the role you played
as Mother,
I am delayed by happy trivia,
ragged bits and pieces
stuffed in envelopes of memory
and wrapped with bright ribbons
of my girlhood and yours.

It is the unshared ones
I need to ferret out from
boxes tightly sealed and shoved
far back in musty corners
before I was born.
If there are ribbons,
I think they may be black.

THE OLD FASHIONED PHONE

I am three and think
the link for me now with the man
who can save me is the big telephone,
the magical box on the wall
at the foot of the steps
that soar up, up and up
to the high second floor
where ghosts or boy cousins
lurk in the dark of the room
I have just fled.

Why has my mother left me
alone in my grandfather's house
with only this phone
I must somehow make work,
let out from its nest
the quick-winged small bird to
fly to my faraway father
and bring his voice to me
caged in this bell-shaped
black thing on a string.

I am teetering on the stair when
my mother bursts in from the yard
and drops to her knees
to cushion my falling.
I cling to her, but only a moment
for look! It is off its hook
dangling and twisting, insisting
I give it a number-please-number
and I proudly begin
the long count to ten.

CONVERSATION WITH MYSELF

How long since I climbed these
mountain-steep steps
to this attic, triangular cage
I played in when the weather was bad?
These bare ribs of wood,
have they shrunk,
become smaller with age?
I must stoop to poke under
the eaves where my doll still sits
at her tea party table.
All right, so I'm taller.
But the lighting up here, is it dimmer?
I remember slivers of sunshine
stuck on the beams.
Does time-layered dust tend
to blend treasures and junk
into colorless gray?

But enough of this chatter
that is taking too much of this day
allotted to clearing my mother's attic.
I am really up here to hunt for
a round-topped creation
of metal and leather
she brought to marriage
for holding lace doilies, fine linens
and her diary with some parts deleted,
a place she would later put things
she never mentioned,
pictures and three baby books,
two never completed.

But why tears? An allergy to dust?
No, I cry at the thought when I sleep
the sleep my mother is sleeping
no one may hunt for my treasures.

Stop sniffling!
One of the four children will.
Still, in this throwaway world
it won't hurt ro remind them
I, too, have a trunk.

PRODUCT OF THE DEPRESSION

Told always to
smile, smile, smile
I watched my mother
pin up the corners of her mouth
each time my father's key
rattled our front door

heard her explain away
red eyes as an old allergy
while the radio warbled
"Happy Days Are Here Again"

paid years later to learn
people have a right
to laugh, to cry.

ON STAGE

Reading with my mother
was live theater,
the big mahogany rocker
our stage,
"The Night Before Christmas"
our longest running play.

Even today, my mother's dramatic
laying a finger on everyone's nose
as Santa rose up the chimney
is family tradition.

Her prim, more refined rendition
that disregarded rime and gave him
a "stomach"
instead of "belly" that
shook like a bowl full of jelly
did not survive
the loosening of time and language.

A CHRISTMAS I DO NOT
LIKE TO REMEMBER

I do not envy the rich
or favored only child
this time of year.
I recall too well
tears at the age of nine
as I sit center stage
like a porcelain doll
amid piles of wrinkled paper
and crinkled ribbons.

Loaded with gifts
and tissue paper guilt,
I am aware
under this same tree
the gift for my mother
is a cook pot
wrapped in brown paper,
the handle sticking out.

TWO CHARACTERS I WISH
I'D NEVER MET AS A CHILD

ALICE

I wish I'd never met you, Alice,
nor your silly friends.
Erect eared rabbits,
grinning cats,
big mouthed frogs
never talked to me
the gibberish you made
a habit of using.
I did not find your
wonderland amusing:
I thought something
was wrong with me
instead of you.

BEN HUR

I liked to drink well water
from longhandled tin dippers
until I saw close movie shots
of your face and lips,
cosmetically bleached and parched,
as you dragged your body
across the desert sand.
I wondered why
the long white arm and hand from
Heaven reached down
a dipper full of water
for only you
there among the bones.

IN THE HIGH SCHOOL LOCKER ROOM

I bruised easily.
An incidental bump
against a chair and the mark
was there, purple and sinister.
I often hid behind long sleeves
until the color faded,
sometimes pretended
it was my monthly period --
the excuse my mother said
she used for skipping gym.

In the locker room that day
the girl dressing next to me
wanted to swap stories
about our healing wounds,
showed me her discolored upper arm,
explained almost proudly
her father beat her
only when he was drunk.

I was glad the bell rang when it did.
Would she have believed my tale
about the chair?
Would I have dared brag about
a gentle father who did not drink
except an eggnog at Christmas --
and coffee, black?

TOT, 3, CAUGHT IN 4-STORY FALL

A dozen years have passed
since you dangled
like loose spaghetti
on the apartment ledge
while your family slept.
What lured you outside --
a noisy pigeon
on the telphone wire,
its white wings properly furled
for balance,
claws neatly curled?
Do you remember
the voice of the stranger
four stories below calling
turn loose, let go,
promising to catch you?

And he did, his arms spread out
taut and precisely right
for the catch a thousand times more
newsworthy than any football
hero's score.

You are fifteen now
that bumbling age
when young humans teeter
on the edge of growing up.
If some bleak day
you are drawn again to the
same window, remember
pigeons learn to fly.

ON DOWN THE LINE

Females in our family
share a tendency to giggle
at inappropriate times:

In the back seat of Mr. Johnson's car
as it jerked and snorted
my mother and me to town

In church, if the buxom soprano
missed the high note
she was laboring to reach

At a wedding reception when dry ice
kept the blocks of ice cream
too hard to cut and guests left unfed

The same way with my daughter
and me, and now with hers:
giggles wiggle to the surface,
harmless as worms giving
birth to butterflies,
embarrassing in our eyes
as our slips showing
or lipstick on our teeth.

ON LIVING IN A GLASS HOUSE

Since my mother believed in sunshine,
the new house built when I was ten
had so many windows
small wall space was left
for furniture and things
handed down for years.

My mother thrived on
sights and sounds our windows
let come in and I remember laughter
always bouncing through them
like balls to be caught
and then returned.

She relished the ritual
of window washing with vinegar
and crumpled old newspapers
saved up for months,
took pride in curtain hanging
and the final adjustment of dusted
green roller shades
she'd let zap to the window tops
to flap and rattle.

But when that inevitable time came
and the house went up for sale,
it stayed on the market
a long, long while.
Too many windows to wash
and buy drapes for,
too much glass, they said,
in case the neighborhood changed.

THE WATERING CAN

My mother, a splendid wisp of
Southern womanhood with opinions
strong and long as Time,
admitted a fullblown dislike
for any flowers
that needed tending.

I remember only the stalwart ones
my father grew and brought inside
as a bud-vase rose,
a camellia or two for a round
crystal bowl or yellow daffodils
stuck in a cut glass pitcher
without further arranging.

She traced her strange bias
to when she was seven
and her new step-mother
thrust a watering can
into her unwilling hands,
putting her in charge forever
of a vast array of plants,
three tiers high
in the bay window
in the cold parlor.

Over the next seventy years,
my mother grew into a joyful
nurturer of people.
She never did make peace
with the watering can.

MY HOUSEPLANTS

My addiction began with the monster
our daughter brought home from college
when it took over her dormitory room.
Like a parent whose children came late in life,
I cling to this motley array of house plants,
bring them in at the first shiver of winter,
arrange for plant sitters when we vacation.

The space they occupy is worth more
than tags they'd wear at a yard sale.
Prospective buyers would spurn
this venerable philodendron
and this nameless plant whose thin leaves
droop like wet ribbons
in imitation of a weeping willow.
I remember when my friend Mary
brought it to me.
The florist shop is out of business now
but it lives on healthy as our friendship.
These cactus plants, tough as the old west
and desert they must yearn for,
I still insist on watering
as often as I do the thirsty ones.

Come fall and our new but smaller house
is done, I must play god,
decide which ones to leave behind
to cope, I hope.

AFTER NEWSPAPER ACCOUNTS OF
RESCUE OF CHILD FROM OLD WELL

There are Jessica wells all over
and trapped children
crying.
But where are the diggers?
These small abused ones
wedged in deep cups of poverty
and neglect
have festering bruises, too.
Unlike small, brave Jessica,
they do not know nursery rimes
their mothers taught them
to sing in the dark
or have reason to expect
someone trying to bring them up.

REACTION TO OLD PICTURE OF
SMALL CHILD SHELLING CORN

Children used to know
where things come from
like milk from cows
instead of bottles
you have to wash
or don't.

They had a chance
to watch things
begin from seeds
planted inside earth
they helped dig,
to welcome with adults
the darkening of clouds
or, if skies stayed blue,
to hold the hose
or fill small buckets
with well or spigot water.

Children watched things
grow and die -- go full circle
from seed to stalwart green
and then to withered stalk
and dry corn cob subject
to their fingers' will.

Too often today's children
grow up thinking popcorn
is born inside a glass cage
at the movies.

RECALLING LITERATURE AND LIFE

He that hath wife and children hath given
hostages to fortune, for they are
impediments to great enterprises,
either of virtue or mischief.

Sir Francis Bacon
17th Century Sage

A fie on you, Sir Francis Bacon.
May you fry in your own words
that stir in me this pot of wrath.
Poppycock, I say. The likes of you,
required reading in my day,
made it harder for girls
to walk past the local YMCA
where boys, wet from swimming nude,
stood out front waiting for their mothers,
britches sometimes twitching,
their eyes switching from girl
to blooming girl.

It was in Miss Mathews' class
you got your "come uppance",
as we used to say down South.
I remember how she'd fling her head,
purse her mouth and sniff in derision
at that very passage I quote
and in retaliation fail to
take points off girls' grades
who dared to spell your first name
with an "e" instead of "i".

IN MEMORY OF
TEACHER/POET ANNE NEWMAN

As I hobble about
for two more awkward weeks
leaning on this borrowed cane,
I remember how deft
you were for years with yours.
In your hand, it was a wand that let
you make things happen
which would not
if you had chosen bed instead.

As I stumble, grumbling
at dropped papers my cane tries
to gather to me, I recall
your unembarrassed laughter
on that writer's conference night
when your notes flew the podium,
scattering on the floor like feathers.

Now that your stride is unwavering
as your will always was,
what about your cane?
Does it remain useless
against a wall somewhere,
bereft of that same guiding hand
so many unsure poets and friends
still need?

ANXIOUS MOTHER

This scientist
eager to discover why things wiggle
and how stars and earth hook together.

This architect
who sharpens pencils with his teeth,
designs houses that look alike and
always with a chimney.

This doctor
who sticks bandaids on everything
but still thinks the best medicine
is a kiss.

This poet who already speaks
in imagery and rhythm
clear as mountain water
flowing up and over
stones in the way.

Can I be sure
his first grade teacher's wonder
is still as fresh as his
and that her wings
do not already droop
from too much paperwork?

WHY I LEFT IT IN THE ANTIQUE SHOP

I almost bought one today
in an antique shop
but reason and the price
finally held sway over
the pull of the past.
But the memory of First Grade
where Miss McMahon assigned me
the first desk I would write on
was strong.

I sniffed the oily polish
on the gently sloped top
and ran my finger in the groove
meant to stop pencils from rolling.
And a hole, yes, a hole
for a round bottle of ink
long after the swirls
and the twirls of fine penmanship
ceased to be taught.

I might have bought it
except for the thought
as I looked at it there:
old time school desks
were never meant to be alone
but hooked all together
in orderly rows
of cast iron and wood
and facing the front
where Miss McMahon stood.

CONFESSION OF A WOMAN WHO THOUGHT SHE'D RATHER BE PRETTY THAN FUNNY

I am three days from thirteen
when the dream I nurture
of my grand entrance into womanhood
bursts --
its shiny expectation of
instant poise and beauty shattered,
its jigsaw pieces scattered over the floor
of the La Petite Elite.

Hidden by the high back of the end booth
of this quite ordinary hangout
of the after school bunch
I am sipping a fountain Coke.
Three gangly boys,
voices slipping in and out of gear,
begin a discussion of girls
they will not ask to the eighth grade prom.
Their reasons are valid ones such as
too many freckles,
too large a nose
or too small breasts.
I freeze when they speak my name:

      "There's Grace."

      "Yeah."

      "You could take Grace."

      "Yeah. She's not good looking
      but she's a lot of fun."

The prom matter settled and their drink
with its three straws noisily consumed,
they leave unaware I was there.

Bereft of my dream,
I know my phone will ring.
And it does --
often.
Still I weep.

It is two decades before I can cherish
the truth of that day in the highback booth.
I stand outside in the hall
and listen to our youngest son dictate
his life story to his kindergarten teacher:
        "Now tell me, David,
          what your family does together."

        "We laugh a lot."

BEHAVIOR IN A STORM

When a crazy knife of lightning
with its thunderbolt handle
splits the sky and the oak out front,
there is a moment
before we cease to be statues,
start fiddling with the blankness
of TVs and lamps.
Startled children
cling to our knees and
refuse to go back to bed.

This is no time
for adherence to rules
but rather the spreading of wings.
We gather our trembling young to us
and head for the nest
aware how much smaller it is
since the last time
weather wrapped us together.

ONLY CHILD

Alone
in the big double bed
of my childhood,
I would pretend
the three aunt-sewn quilts
that pinned me to the mattress
with the weight
of their cross-stitched patches
were really heavy casts.
I strained to lift my thin legs
(broken perhaps in a daring
but ill fated leap of my horse
in the Camden Cup races).
I smiled wanly at friends bringing
bunches of handpicked violets
and boxes of Whitman's Sampler.
I was no longer alone
in my big double bed waiting
for leg cramps or sleep
to free me
from my patchwork of guilts.

MR. JAKE

Mr. Jake was thought to be
most wise about the weather.
He could lick one finger
and with it raised and slowly turning
predict whether or not the wind
was right for sailing.

If Mr. Jake was spotted
on his morning stroll,
a black umbrella swinging
from the crook of his arm,
mothers took precautions - -
closed windows before they left,
brought clothes in from the line
and told children to stay off the lake
even though the sky was clear.

On those days when Mr. Jake
chose to stay indoors and
complained of aching joints,
a cold front was surely due
and good cooks knew to allow
more time for homemade bread to rise.

The surprise was the time
his actions predicted sun
and gentle breezes from the south.
Instead, a storm ripped out of nowhere,
tilted our sailboats
like saucers on their sides,
whipped our mothers' skirts
tight as flags around wet poles
as they stood on the dock straining
to will us children back to shore.

Abruptly as it started,
wind and rain stopped,
boats righted, nose counts
came out right.
Yet things never were quite the same.
What mattered now was that
handmade quilts put confidently
out to sun got soaking wet,
their borders that had thrashed
against the ground ripped and tattered,
mute testimony to Mr. Jake's
mistake about the weather.

Folks began paying more attention
to the daily paper,
to their Atwater Kent radios
and the fellow on KDKA predicting
the weather due in Pittsburg.

As for Mr. Jake,
he continued to moisten
a finger on request
but on his morning stroll
he always carried his umbrella
and walked as though
his bones were aching.

HORSE AND BUGGY

Buggy Hit by Auto
Killing Amish Man, 20
                    AP Headline

I also worry about the horse,
imagine its frantic snorts
as the reins go slack
and a wooden shaft digs into
its heaving, glistening side.
The buggy can be repaired.
Neighbors would be skilled
at putting buggies back together.

But what about the horse?
Can it feel confident again
to clip-clop in rhythmic ease
along the street or wait patiently
outside the village store?
Or must it be put away to graze,
live out its nervous days and nights
in pastures still too close
to unpenned metal monsters.

I write about the horse
but, oh, the Amish mother!

SIRENS ON ROUTE 276

Two cars brutalize each other,
turn carefully waxed metal
into grotesque art, craze
no-shatter glass in geometric patterns
and fling occupants like rag dolls
against roadside trees and grass.

There is a moment of quiet
before the noise begins.

Police cars roar up,
security in lights
that blink unsynchronized.
Rescue sirens wail their coming and
mothers check to see
if teenagers are in.

THE MENDER

You always did live outside
your fragile bag of bones and skin
so after bed and fluffed pillows
laid early claim to it,
instead of crying,
you made laughter your wings
and we kept on bringing to the nest
cracked pieces of our lives
for you to mend while we slept.

MISS BESSIE

Miss Bessie had a poet's touch
with her crochet needle,
especially during the last
of her many years
already gone past eighty
when we became neighbors and friends.

She called the bright colored circles
she created pot-holders
but I called them Miss Bessie's poems.
I have two dozen or more,
and seeing how they brighten
up my kitchen it occurs to me
they would go nicely as ornaments to hang
on Heaven's Christmas tree this year.

In case her crochet needle
and big bag filled with balls of yarn
she always kept beside her chair
count as earthly possessions,
she might be supplied instead
with a streak of gold lightning
or the silver line of a falling star
and bright rainbows for yarn.
I have a feeling that Miss Bessie,
relieved now of pain and
a certain loneliness old age often brings,
will get right to work and crochet
a thousand pot holder-ornaments
by Christmas day.

POINT OF VIEW

In my book,
I can not lump the Sixties
into one stinking bag of trash
dragged to history's
landfill and dumped.

Too much of my mothering
was done in those scary
years of change
when the telephone beside our bed,
ignoring time zones,
shrilled us awake with its ringing,
bringing across its high thin lines
chunks of our children's lives:

>"Speaking in Spanish
>is not so great
>but the Peace Corps is..."

>"Heading West to work
>in fields to learn what
>it is to really sweat..."

>"Riding box cars to
>Arizona to test the wind,
>see how hoboes live."

In these current, flaccid Nineties
when flag waving parades are back,
I keep transposing to my television
screen undaunted teens marching with
homemade freedom banners,
placards of hope.

OWNERS OF A VINTAGE TV

Accustomed as we are
to digesting our nightly news
in generic black and white,
we are sometimes startled,
only slightly amused,
when motels or friends
force-feed us on their sets.
We feel uneasy to find
how soon our own eyes
adapt to unrealities
of color they swallow
without a blink.

Do subtle word distortions
also slip by the sentinels
we think the mind should be?

ADVENT AT A FRIEND'S HOUSE
for Faye, November 29, 1987

We shall not soon forget, if ever,
this celebrating at your home --
nine people, comfortable around
a table meant for six,
drinking wine and cider,
eating homemade soup
and breaking bread together:
cornbread from a mix
and nutbread mother-made
and sent by mail and love
a day ahead.

We found a closeness of spirit
and mind around your table
in celebration of the coming
of the same Christ we all claim
in slightly different ways.
Here at your table
we found ourselves sharing
laughter and almost-tears
as we told of high hopes
and fears of newness we face --
younger parents
who find their houses
too big when, by choice,
children are waved off to college;
and the plight of older parents
who feel embraced and welcomed
as we build another nest
but find ourselves flying

from steeple to church steeple
in search of that elusive thread
we need for tying it together
on Sundays in a new place.

How joyfully this night
we celebrated the past,
the oldness of familiar hymns
you played so skillfully
you drew us into singing,
our voices perhaps not as much
in tune as were our hearts
as we then stood together,
nine of us, arms entwined
in the new-old ritual
of saying goodbye to friends.

WIFE TRYING TO KEEP AWAKE
IN TOO HOT ROOM

This is not a matter of boredom.
I think stopping stream pollution
is a worthy cause.
I feel every effort must be made to find
a solution to acid rain,
the plight of the gopher turtle
and the alligators in the Everglades.
Every effort must be made
in the area of energy.
But the amount I am using to keep my eyes behaving
is of more interest to me at this moment
than what turned off airconditioners are saving.

STALKING THE SUNDAY CLASSIFIEDS

In this vast morass of gnat-size print,
dry poets thirsty for themes for poems
and women on the prowl for bargains
hunt religiously.

The latter, car keys ready,
may phone-check
before they light out after
prey to mount as trophies
or stuff in closets
for their own yard sales.

We poets, stalking the same dense area,
hope not to leave our desks
to capture now and then
a cracked or limping dream
compressed
in twenty words or less.

ZACCHEUS BRINGS HOME GUESTS

I feel for Zaccheus' wife
that day her tree climbing,
tax collector husband
bursts into the house
to announce guests arriving
any minute
-- at least one
to sleep the night.

"Guests!" she cries,
eyes flicking
from floor to table
with dishes unwashed.
Womanlike, she starts
to sweep,
complaining about not
a thing in the house
to eat or drink.
Seeing how disheveled and
scratched her sweaty husband is,
she suggests he wash and change.
She will fix the bed.

"But wait . . .
who is this guest?
Surely not that Jesus fellow,
the one who tries to talk
Godfearing Jews to give away
their money?

"Isn't he the one who
hangs around with
not just the hungry
but harlots and other sinners?

"Well, all I have to say is I hope
he won't bring with him
that loose woman who washes feet
and dries them with her hair.

"Oh, Zaccheus,
what will the neighbors think?"

MARY

I see you as child-woman first,
fresh as spring rain and in love
with a boy-man his pals call Joe,
the one you must gently remind,
in case he forgets, that this son
every man dreams of spawning
will not be his.

Being woman, and wife,
it is easy for me to visualize
the plan you devise for the telling.
You pick a bright morning
the clear night has predicted,
rise early, knead the risen dough
and feed the clay oven scraps
of wood, pieces of cedar and olive,
laying the longer sticks crosswise
on top to tease the coals to flame.
When the loaves are fragrant and brown,
the fresh caught fish tender,
then you will call him
to come and eat and listen.

As wife and mother, I share
your pain and pride on
that sabbath when your boy-now-twelve
stands in the tabernacle to announce
he will not follow in his father's profession,
will let the adz and saw, the plane lie unused
while he goes about his father's work.
I can imagine other parents
crowding around you and Joseph,
calling it adolescent rebellion,
the first sign of growing up.
But you know different, Mary.

I can not walk in your sandals
for this next scene, Mary.
As mother of three grown sons
I can not pretend fitting the passive role
Mideastern women even now
might expect to play
on that blasphemous day when Pilate,
washing his hands of the whole affair,
signals the slow death walk to begin.

I see myself flinging
the covering cloth from my face and head,
rushing to try to ease the weight of the wood,
making a spectacle of myself
yelling at the jeering, spitting crowd
as I claw at the cross dropping in its hole,
jerk at the skirts of those whose work it is
to hammer nails into flesh of my flesh,
all the while crying, calling on the Lord
to do something,
and being surprised when He does.

I take myself out of this scene, Mary,
leave the stage to you
and to the irate Father
who in His wrath and hurt
thunders the heavens to awesome darkness,
drenches the land and the scrambling crowd
with His tears
and breaks open the black sky
to spotlight a wet hill with its crosses
and you and two other mothers
keeping watch.

SPELLING LESSON

I was five, going on six
as they used to say,
the day my mother, gently
and patiently as the teacher
running pump water over the hand
of the child blind,
spelled out d-e-a-t-h
in the palm of my mind.

An only child hearing the first time
of two small brothers dead,
one before her and one after,
I did not cry at the telling,
reacted instead with silly laughter
at my two forearms stuck
to the cold oilcloth
of the kitchen table.

Later, when I was eight
going on nine,
my best friend and I had contests
to see who could cry real tears first
or go longest without lips
cracking in a smile.
I always won by thinking back
to the day when I was five and learned
to be born does not mean
always to be alive.

NIGHT SITTER

I do not know your name,
only that for one stark December week
you kept watch while my father slept,
sharing the shadow hours with my mother
that ought to be mine to remember.

I ask myself how can a daughter,
only flesh and blood left
of a mother perched on the brink of dying,
know how to divide the bread of her
own life into the proper number of pieces
to feed them all --
four small children aware only
that plants and kittens die,
and a tired husband trying to fill
the gaps of absence but also hungry.

Were you surprised that night you came
to sit and found me in charge?

What did you think
when you slipped into her room
already quiet with the breath of Death
and found the small bowl of mush uneaten,
tried to feed her, gently cooing, coaxing
the spoon between her slackened lips?

When you emerged from her room, bright-eyed,
offering us the half-teaspoon of hope in your hand,
did you understand her doctor and her daughter
no longer believed in miracles?

FUNERAL ARRANGEMENTS

I am trying to explain
to the men in black suits
their start-to-finish package,
including choice of silk lining
for burying boxes,
does not fit my mother.
She always dragged me
up and down the stairs
of Smith's Department Store
to avoid confining elevators.

The offer to transport, for a nominal fee,
all the floral offerings to the site in the next town
will not be needed
since she requested no flowers.
My mother felt flowers
were meant to grow outside
not bent to pretty shapes with wire.

The music suggested is too solemn for one
who loved to dance, admitting
she slipped out from her Baptist oriented home
every chance she found
to kick up her heels.

I wish there had been the option
of picking a sunny day to have her ashes flown
through the spaciousness of sky
with white clouds in bloom
and only wind making music.
I think the freedom and the beauty
of the flight would have outweighed
my mother's lifelong fear of heights.

EPILOGUE

If this Victrola of memory
on which I keep playing
old records should break,
the needle stuck and going
round and round and round
in the same groove,
I hope the sound is
my mother and me
laughing.

Yet, I sometimes wish that
in the last clear weather
of my mother's living
we had cried together
letting held back tears gush out
like a rain filled river
flooding the thirsty sheets,
wetting her gown, my blouse,
soaking our hair and our faces,
two women no longer wearing
happy masks to protect each other.

I guess any woman called mother
who has three times felt
her own water break
releasing long-wanted babies
and later knelt beside
the graves of two
would be afraid of drowning
if she wept.

ABOUT THE AUTHOR

Grace Beacham Freeman grew up in South Carolina and graduated from Converse College. Although her writing experience covers many fields, she has concentrated since 1969 on contemporary poetry. This is her fourth book in this genre. She was Poet Laureate of South Carolina in 1985-1986 and is known for her readings of her current as well as her earlier, more traditional poetry. Since 1987, she and her husband have lived at Brevard, NC, where she continues an active schedule of writing and readings.

ABOUT THE ARTIST

Charles Loftin lives in Denton, NC, and works for Burlington Industries. He is primarily involved with the Davidson County Art Guild. He speaks of himself as an active preservationist. Loftin's drawing on the cover is in the art collection of Elizabeth Verner Hamilton of Charleston.

ABOUT THE BOOK

Grace Freeman's earlier trilogy reflected a progressive maturing of the author breaking through to freedom from the barriers experienced during childhood and youth. In THIS WOMAN CALLED MOTHER she examines recollections from her childhood, youth and early adult years for clues to the mystery as to just who mother, anyone's mother, is as an adult human, not simply as nurturer. The journey has taken many twists and turns for a number of years.

SOUTH CAROLINA STATE LIBRARY

0 01 01 0147842

DUE DA

Layout and design by John's Press
Printing and manufacture by Christopher's Press in
Fayetteville, North Carolina